Something Else's Thoughts

Printed in the United States of America

ISBN-13: 978-1-946460-05-9

Library of Congress Control Number: 2018946278

Published by **Transcendent Zero Press**, 2018.
For more information, please visit our website at
www.transcendentzeropress.org.

Something Else's Thoughts is © Dah / Transcendent Zero Press, 2018. No portion of this book may be reproduced in any form, whether electronic or in print, without expressed consent of the author or of the publisher. This edition is back and white interior.

Dustin D. Pickering, publishing correspondent:
Editor@transcendentzeropress.org

Cover Graphics and Design: © Dah 2018. all rights reserved.

FIRST EDITION
Transcendent Zero Press

Something Else's Thoughts

DAH

Transcendent Zero Press
Houston, TX

for

Ron Tompkins

*Are dreams memories
or are memories dreams?*

Table Of Contents

Introduction
by Michael Grotsky

Proem

Broken / 17

Part One: Symbolism

Misdirected / 21

Wherever I Was / 22

Myth / 23

Language / 24

Part Two: Imperfection

Disheveled Boats / 27

I Say Dream Only / 28

The Ash Between Light And Dark / 29

The Hard Tumble / 30

So The Day Is This / 31

Swirl Of Holy Ghost / 32

The Balance Between / 33

Illusions Proceed / 34

Everyday Motion / 35

Weather Predicts Everything / 36

Suddenly No Light / 38

Without Voice Without Living / 39

Pass Through The Center / 40

Imperfection / 41

The Vanishing Of Differences / 42

The Silence Of A Kiss / 43

Part Three: Beyond Time

Point Of Completion / 47

The Progress Of Life / 48

A Clock Appears / 49

Never A Sky Clear Enough / 51

We Turn Into Earth / 52

Night Has Fallen, Aged / 53

Beyond Slumber / 54

Words Of Dreams / 55

A Place Beyond Time / 56

Part Four: The Key Holders

The Drunkenness In Its Eyes / 59

Transformative Motion / 61

The Murderer Of Fish / 63

Nobody Looks At Us / 65

Omni Everything / 68

Little By Little / 69

Something Else's Thoughts / 70

Been Dreaming Too Long / 71

Somewhere In My Head / 72

The Key Holders / 74

Part Five: The Way

The Way / 77

Cross-Legged In Meditation / 79

The Box / 80

Clouds Rub Against It / 82

A Colorless Prism / 83

As If Only Beginning / 85

Motion Unknown / 86

Above The Universe / 87

Every Dream Is A Crowded World / 88

Part Six: Incomplete

Empty You, Empty Me / 91

REM / 95

A Living Gray / 96

My Indignity, My Delusion? / 97

Broken #2 / 98

Incomplete / 99

Part Seven: Therapy / 103

Part Eight: Dreams / 111

Acknowledgements

Author

Introduction

I first met Dah in 1998 when he was expressing himself in photographic images that were poetic, mysterious, erotic, and dreamy. These images are of concrete things, like Venetian masks, women and seascapes, that reveal abstract ideas moving between dreaming and waking while suggesting something beneath and beyond the subjects in his camera lens.

Along the line Dah's photographs morphed into poems that speak of nature, desire, loss, and, of course, dreams. They speak of confusion and difficulty in distinguishing between sleeping and waking, love and lust, and, as the muse in *Something Else's Thoughts* says, "Death, the forgotten comfort"

In short, Dah skates along the invisible line that moves between these states and leaves us wondering what exactly is this line, where does it come from, and who controls it? If it's shifting then how do we distinguish between reality and dreams? Is there a difference? Is this madness or simply the existential dilemma that constitutes and defines our lives?

In the poem "Imperfection" Dah laments: "along the way I've misplaced my guardian angel and between life and death the gray line expands." He admits in "Words Of Dreams", "the frankness about my spiritual poverty: I own nothing of myself not the acceptance nor the resistance." And from "We Turn Into Earth" he asserts: "the world will pass and the gray line continues, like an eternal suture inside the soul." Then in "Broken #2" he questions: "Can I exist like this, can anyone live this way knowing that within our minds a sub-mind of deep surveillance creates eyes inside one's privacy?"

Ambitious in its scope, *Something Else's Thoughts*, Dah's seventh book of the decade, is a rumination on desire, loss, absence, and death, as he weaves one poem into the next, creating a tale that walks the high wire of love and disorder between the narrator and his muse, who contributes to the experience. They inhabit a nebulous world that slips between, behind, under, and into "the gray line" — a metaphor that runs throughout this work as a mystifying and elusive divide between all things.

But *the gray line* is not merely a marker between events; at times it takes on an active, aggressive role, threatening the protagonist and his muse.

In a state of menace *the gray line* is an aggressor seizing its victims, wrapping itself around a leg, "looking for completion", or pulling to the bottom of the sea a pelican's carcass, or harassing Mr. Serling of the Twilight Zone, and even downing a jet which disappears without a trace.

In "REM", Dah defines *the gray line's* intent: "to suck negative ions from the water, to suck them from our bodies, to keep us melancholic, confused, and submissive." It is "the ambiguous region between two conditions, containing trace features of both." It is a "place beyond time" where we find "the vanishing of differences." It is the anti-hero of the story.

Within this bizarre dreamscape there is also dark humor. In "Pass Through The Center" the poet plays with the gray line: "I take the gray line and hang it from ceiling to floor, taut as a bow string, and use a broom handle to stroke it, like a cellist, until sound waves roll from side to side."

But the line that separates us from psychosis is also thin and fragile. In the poem "Imperfection" Dah writes: "If memories and dreams are voiceless then what is it I'm hearing? And then he states, "at times I feel nobody's home, that my body is soulless and everything's a dead dream."

Then, with his muse, the narrator seeks rejuvenation along the coast, where *the gray line* divides solid and liquid: "I must return to the coast, to the sea's purity, to the infinite way." It is there at the coast that narrator and muse seek refuge in one another, in passion, in the fact of flesh. The muse attempts to ground the narrator, who slips between coherency and ambiguity. In the title poem, "Something Else's Thoughts", Dah writes: "We are two parts of gray's polarities: the simple and complex, the sound soundless, black white. Should I speak or should I listen?"

In "A Place Beyond Time' he asks: "How does one make sense of what is ambiguous?" And from "Been Dreaming Too Long" he inquires: "will only gray remain after the universe dies?"

On which side of the line do we stand? This is a question only we can decide for ourselves, and when we are consumed by *Something Else's Thoughts*, decisions are never final.

Michael Grotsky

Montreal, Canada
February 2018

Is all that we see or seem
but a dream within a dream?

– E. A. Poe

Proem

Broken

That which is broken works
for those who want it broken

Walking the city in this August dawn
my thirst
a cracked basin
This emotional thirst
the city's grime

I drag the gray line behind me
The homeless snigger
at this misfortune

shaky breath

crowded thoughts

conflicting voices

gray divergence

breakdown

I must return to the coast
to the sea's purity
to the infinite way

Part One

Symbolism

Misdirected

No one understands
how dark erases light
Some call it old skin

Moon is born blind
like the insides of caves
A cave is hot
like the middle of a throat

Then there's the gray line
between life and death
earth, water
salt and sea

I've understood this for many lives
though I cannot remember
the bodies before me
Their voices, a molt of myth

I do not understand how
feelings attack nerves
how one season consumes the other
or the day's periphery that lightens
then darkens and
what reasons are there for truth
if truth is misdirected

Knowing then not knowing
Confucius or Confusion

Wherever I Was

Dying can be painful
Death
absolute as in
I once lived

Wherever I was
am
Creation was
is
always

I move my eyes along
a sudden flight of swallows
and I often seek rest

Though there's nothing
in rest

Death, a hollow sound

Myth

The sea does not call
this is myth

Low tide is food
air caresses
pliable

A ripple knows nothing
dissolves
The thinnest puddle of clouds
reflections

Tracing sand with a finger
I wish upon a secret
Truth
Always
Nothing else

Language

Before language there were
sound-drifts
grunts, groans, whimpering

There was imagination
not yet imagined
Wishes became spells of wickedness
something dark

Language was an embryo unfurling
in caves
spores of guttural seeds
spit into syllables
The white glue of saliva
held them together

Slowly, language spoke
The future
a word-heavy albatross

Regret is not light

                              She asks: Is drifting dark?

To drift is to know the meaning
of loneliness

Part Two

Imperfection

Disheveled Boats

Tonight a fast wind tangles the waves
making sounds like distant chants
Breaker after breaker gone wild

The current, a jealous lover
that pulls apart, together, apart,
a net of salt, in, out, floating

                    She says: To float is divine

Our bodies, disheveled boats moored
against the sand
A sky of gulls roving, roving
Restless watchers

We sink into sultry heat
and fuck in the dunes

Her black hair, night spills
an apparition
A cantilever of darkness balances
the ornate moon

We are fire and sea, undulant
floating driftwood, lyrical,
something of a hymn
Dune grass rises between our thighs

She curls beneath me like waves coming
one after another
Saltwater trickles down the dune
White-hot Marrow-hot
breaking waves

I Say Dream Only

It starts to cloud, heavy gray clouds
then begins to rain
Drops the length of drumsticks

The tin roof on a beach shack
is a tight percussive skin
that rises off-pitch
Dune grasses sway
to the drumming
flap to the beat
The waves applaud

We take refuge in the shack
The storm crashes against the walls

We sleep or should I say dream only
She, a starfish, I, a gray line
Starfish floats, gray line catches

Huddled together on a wooden cot
surrounded by sand, salt, storm
She, a starfish, I, a gray line
I lift her to taste the sea
a clam floats over my tongue
I lift her higher
tasting more of the sea

The Ash Between Light And Dark

At night during the rain
my dreams are wintry still lives
No one is breathing

In morning's glow the gray line
is the ash between light and dark
the middle-world between
life and death
pulling on both sides

because bodies move
then stop
as if collective matter is cruel

                    She says: All bodies turn into trees
                               bones to roots
                               skin to trunks
                               hands to leaves

                               all seamen turns to oceans

                               Some believe that
                               we know how to follow death
                               to the covenant of purity
                               to the absence of language

                               They say: Without worry
                               we know how to journey
                               to the other side

The Hard Tumble

Life's fleeting moments
inflate, deflate
hungry then full

Change, the conveyance
that sprouts into sadness
grows into silence
a seclusion of sorrow

Where have they all gone
those who have broken out early

                    She whispers: You must stop being
                            the hard tumbling wind
                              that chokes itself until frozen

So The Day Is This

Lifeline, flat-line, horizon line
the sun's balancing point

I dreamt this last night
If now this is reality
then life is a manifestation of dreams

Fleeting moments: the red line
burning bush
Haven't seen her for years

So the day is this, closing.

On the grass, a fallen yellow leaf
asks for a longer lifeline

A green hummingbird, one last drink

The sun flat-lines

The gray line binds me, a subterranean tendril
At first its movements are tender

Swirl Of Holy Ghost

The gray line, a band around Earth
that separates daylight from darkness
A shifting line, scientifically known as
The Twilight Zone

Radio propagation along the gray line
is extremely efficient

The voice from the radio, a Tight-Mind,

enthusiastically announces: Jesus Will Save You!
                      But first you must denounce the flesh,
                      fornication, booze and drugs.
                      Denounce worldly things and let Jesus in
                      and keep your heart on the Heavenly
                      Afterlife.

I lift a joint to my mouth
and inhale the Herb of Salvation
then exhale
a Swirling Holy Ghost

            Enthusiastic Evangelist: Jesus will pour into you
                      then pour from you
                      from within Brothers and Sisters
                      The Light will shine
                      Seek Salvation Now!

The gray line wraps around the radio
I listen for the crossover. Static.
High-pitched squeal. The voice,
garbled, terminated.
Oh, heavenly afterlife!

The Balance Between

At the margin along fog and sea
the line is like a photoengraving
only now it blends with gray

> She asks: Then the gray line is the balance
> between life and death
> and from this rises heaven?

Suddenly the wind,
a rush of winter. Sand,
the harpoons of space
stinging like nettle

We run for cover
along the narrow paths between coastal sages

A flock of starlings take the sky
only to dive down
to strip the berries
from nearby bushes

Pressed together, a percussive pulse between us
I unbutton her shirt and like a starling
savor her dark berries. Our bodies shift
so her skirt lifts
and my grazing hardness
finds its way between the savage obedience
of her thighs

This is the moisture that steams
into breathlessness

The sand-infested wind whips our skin
the gray line slinks excitedly around us
Oh, heavenly rise!

Illusions Proceed

Oncoming winter pulls, drags
Sky, a charcoaled entity
mournful, teary-eyed

Standing on the gray line
between two seasons,
a littered trail
of autumn's torment
Dark moon, a blown bulb

                      She asks: In age, or maybe in length
                              how long is the gray line?
                              Does its weight vary?

I'm not hesitant to say
it's intricate
The gray line seeks expansive attachment
a point of unraveled mastery over thoughts

This knowledge is for imagination

To imagine the gray line is to understand your death
a slow uncorking of chardonnay

                      She whispers: Death, the forgotten comfort

Really what the gray line covets
is complete ascendancy
There will be dominance from it
aided by the Tight-Minds
who abuse it

Suddenly the rain becomes language
pressuring our skin. The atmosphere
is writing in wet-cursive about perfection
and imperfection

Everyday Motion

Perfection and imperfection
a storytelling favorite
the fable of
yes and no, good, bad

We spin in between
sometimes dominated by one
The gravitational pull
wants to bury us
ego wants to expand

In everyday motion
we attempt to implement perfection:
the perfect body
perfect mind
perfect lover

Dark light in its perfection
Bright light in its perfection
both imperfect to the other

Tonight I feel imperfect
tossing and turning at the surface
of discomfort
because perfection is a con
a phony
a shopkeeper for the misinformed

Weather Predicts Everything

February, a seemingly endless squall
I'm on a Denver to Utica Greyhound

With winter crusading its deepest faith
I take a seat in the back. Sleep most of the trip
Occasionally I'm jolted awake by the driver's
announcements or the long gasp of air brakes
at small-town terminals

At a time of being awake
the mid-western landscape
turns into a white ocean
except for the abandoned farm vehicles
tractors, balers, tillers, that are ghost ships
Some have sunk beneath the sea

Weather predicts everything:
its strategies, its chaos
its cloud-bruised sky
and dreaming can be reduced to
the moment she boards the bus,
walks the length of the aisle
and sits next to me

With the sun setting, bus lights dimmed,
a new odyssey arises. A college woman
heading back to school. We begin flirting
comparing life-notes. One common ground is
our perception of the gray line between love and sex

Later that evening she excuses herself
and goes into the restroom at the back
then returns wearing a loose skirt and sweater
She sits down, smiles, moves closer to me
and puts her head on my shoulder. The bus is
near empty. We are alone in the back

To enter the gray line is such a situation:
my hand between her thighs,
her hand between mine, our mouths,
moisture, bliss.
Then, at her stop, she vanished

Suddenly No Light

The Twilight Zone
scientifically known as the lowest level of an ocean
which sunlight penetrates

The ambiguous region between
two conditions
containing trace features of both

                      She says: Near *The Twilight Zone*
                          there are nerve-tingling occurrences
                          that could be water-noise
                          or signals buried in our psyche
                          the sound bites of desire and fear

Later as we walk along the coast
breakers are the motion that fuses us
the salt as seasoning
the watery evolution of breathing

Like fish thriving at the surface
we face the light
an explosion transmutes everything
as if perfection were a laughing mask

Suddenly no light
we pass *The Twilight Zone*
heading into the dark

Without Voice Without Living

All night
in between memories and dreams
there are strong signals
coming from the gray line

My heart hammers blood
into my over-loaded veins
and bones are the plaster
holding this statue together

Both memories and dreams
send out instructions
without voice without living
and the thin line between them, the prophet,
the muse, shortens the distance

Are dreams memories
or are memories dreams?

I close my eyes
light dials in
the search engine spins
I'm prepared to learn

Pass Through The Center

I listen for instructions
from the gray line
quiet as a thief, I listen
The gray line flaps in the dark,
like a startled pigeon

All night I've been listening
while the storm rattles the windows
and the shack's frame squeaks
its tired rickshaw sounds

I take the gray line and hang it
from ceiling to floor, taut as a bow string
and use a broom handle to stroke it,
like a cellist, until sound waves roll
from side to side
then pass through the center

It's there, at the center, the instructions
sound: a requiem for white roses,
a German opus, noise of death

My silver hair, like faint diffusers between
Yin and Yang, winter's fog,
Alpine white, frozen
like the hardness of ice

Then I wake up, the hieroglyphs still with me
the code, symbolism, sound bites

Breaking daylight fills everything

Everything is the same as tomorrow.

Imperfection

My head is filled with last night's dreams
or memories or both

At times I want to forget
that with opposites
there's a gray line between them
and for me
creates reasons to not believe in anything

If memories and dreams are voiceless
then what is it I'm hearing

In a dream
stars rose from the ocean
in the midst of that
a bodiless voice
with memories seeking moments
that had vanished

At times I feel nobody's home
that my body is soulless
and everything's a dead dream

Having not fulfilled its life
a dead dream is imperfection
a dog-eared page nobody returns to

Along the way
I've misplaced my guardian angel
and between life and death
the gray line

The Vanishing Of Differences

Because in the beginning
we were without language
this then is the account

We have landed here from the other side
pushed together into clumps

There were words beneath our skin
souls talking
teaching us memories of self

This is how we arrived
with spirits longer than eternity

Because the gray line is without margins
black and white blend
Gray becomes *The Way*
the vanishing of differences

The Silence Of A Kiss

At first, words dropped like pebbles
then stones then boulders
but there was no talk of the gray line

One was guilty or not guilty
even though matters were never cleared
nor resolved

A knock on the unlocked door,
she invites herself in, exclaiming: I want to name the gray line
                                    before others abuse it

                                    Let's call it Clay, as in gray clay
                                    as in clay of earth
                                    as in gray matter, gray mud
                                    mud bath, quicksand, twilight …

I silence her with a kiss
the words wash from her tongue
I lift her tee shirt to the shoulders
then over her head Long black hair
falls loosely Small breasts
soft shells, dark pearls

Lifting her skirt, we fuck standing
and become one breath

One breath
river meets ocean
one breath

Part Three
Beyond Time

Point Of Completion

In the spaces between the four directions
a gray exists for each, the area of uncertainty

North, South, East, West
it's here the gray line nears completion

as in *North By Northwest* where Mr. Grant's character
searches for a point of completion
for his suspicions

Grant is confident that the gray line
between good and bad has been altered
by the story's Antagonist

Grant drags the weight of the gray line
through the story
hiding and lurking until he makes his entry
and exposes the criminality

The Progress Of Life

Of *The Twilight Zone*, Mr. Serling said:
It is the middle ground between light and shadow

The gray line would be of no concern
if I could see it entering, or leaving
or see its other side
or if we spoke the same language
or had the same thoughts, shadows,
or voices

If I knew its shape or its vibration
then I might take chances, real chances
and the progress of life could be less impossible
the game less rigged

Where does thinking find its darkness
or its fear, a fear that is ultimately clever
The gravity of fear, an immense world,
unnatural voices in the middle
from every direction

I feel my bones burning,
a synthesis of air. The gray line
in death, in dust, from dust

I jolt. Her breathing wakes me
I'm conscious in a dubious way
The hour hand, time's cursive
a foreshadowing of seconds

Another breath, motion, the body of a butterfly
hatches in my arms
My lips pluck at her wings

her breathing stops

    I jolt

A Clock Appears

I jolt awake
and see that I am the eye of this dream
Language speaks in ripples

In an empty black room:
Mr. Serling is bound to an armless wooden chair
bound by the gray line, bound tightly
When he struggles, the gray line grows in girth

Mr. Serling is pleading
But I'm deaf and cannot hear him

The room trembles then rains from the floor up,
puddles on the ceiling reflect the gray line

> Mr. Serling asks repeatedly:
> Is this *The Twilight Zone,* is it?
> Help. Oh God, Help …

I can't hear him

Beneath his pristine dark blue suit and tie
the gray line crawls under his skin. A clock appears
in midair. It's 4:21

Leftover smoke heaps into fog
Serling's eyes are cold ash

When the fog clears, his left leg stands alone
in the middle of the chair. It limps
to the edge, trips over the gray line,
disappears

I jolt. Wake up.

I hear the television. There's conversation
about the gray line, the ocean
She's watching *The Twilight Zone*
And from the room I hear gasping, whispering, wet sounds
Sea musk pervades the air

Never A Sky Clear Enough

Like dim, rustic lanterns, eyes crack open
Hazy moment

There's never a sky clear enough to wake me
never a shadow alive enough to be mine

Something steps out of my body
gathers into a gray orb

skin droops, rips
but it's nothing, really

just tissue pulling apart
bones disconnecting
and muscles tearing along a genealogy of millenniums

Exhausted nerves, hours trail off

We Turn Into Earth

I will pass. Yes. We will.
The world will pass
and the gray line continues
like an eternal suture inside the soul

Flesh is sky, ocean.
Breakers carry clouds.
Language is glued to the wind
and swept forward.
Bones: in the image of stars

Wearing fog's drab robe
we walk barefoot over sand
Her black hair lifts, feathers

Lying naked in a dune slack
on a bed of shells,
pelican wings, sea grass
we turn into sand-tapestries
tribal rhythms, earth tones

Her tropical mouth,
fruit, fertility, Eden
Her legs around my waist,
sultry waves

Night Has Fallen, Aged

Ocean, wind
Sand hits our eyes
light kaleidoscopes
Sitting along the water's edge

           She says: I feel that we have forgotten
                    and cannot decide on why
                    or where …

I'm sensing the gray line between us
A living space
of hollowed dreams
the wind in d-sharp minor
ringing in my left ear

           She implies: I think we've lost our way

A young Taoist monk walks barefoot along the water's edge
His feet are feelers
collecting sand dabs
The wind begins to paint

Sticking out of the sand
a jet plane's tail wing, inlaid with rust

She is talking but the ocean is louder
and heavy with the world's blunders
The water flickers like electric divination

Lying in the dunes, I open my eyes
Night has fallen, aged

I pull the severed wings over our nakedness
and tuck in to keep her warm

Beyond Slumber

Open eyes wide wider
there
the gray line above stars
farther than space

Through bright passages and dark passages
my eyes expand and contract
through sleep, beyond slumber

stillness cracks
motion
the gray line shifts
sound bites
the gray line shifts
higher

Words Of Dreams

To forgive echoes their honesty
to forgive shadows their stalking
to forgive dreams their ruckus

Words of dreams:
an insider's talk, the assuming,
the incomplete

I search through books
to understand my uneasiness
to sense my shortcomings
to question:

life's reckless current, trailing off voices
replies I have not given

If I am nothing then I am
a skinless piece of light. The frankness
about my spiritual poverty:

I own nothing of myself
not the acceptance nor the resistance:

I have become the thinnest rain
that has no effect on a drought

A Place Beyond Time

We draw thoughts to the equator
our conversations have no boundaries

                She asks: What do the gray line and the equator
                          have in common?

                She suggests: Invisibility, a place beyond time

We walk out of the dunes
crushing sand dollars beneath our feet
and enter the frigid water

Rinsing sand from our bodies
a discolored jellyfish floats the surface
a wingless pelican drifts by
its lifeless body seeks rest

The gray line wraps around the bird
and takes it to the bottom. Bewildered:

how does one make sense of
what is ambiguous?

Part Four

The Key Holders

The Drunkenness In Its Eyes

A trail of footprints
scorched by the sun
harassed by the wind

Horizon's thin gray streak
is a haunted place

Opaque blue above
crashes of splintered blue below

The careless sweating of clouds
such ancient elixir

Scarlet blood of a hooked fish
is liquid rose, terror flames in its throat

The gray line's impact
from blue to horizon to hooked fish
to the mind's rattling

                              She asks: What are you thinking?

The way dragonflies pile up in the light
not to bend their shapes but to shape their shadows

                              She replies: I love the tenderness
                                        in your thoughts

I'm looking at the fish. Mucous-bubbles ooze
from its gills. The drunkenness in its eyes

The killer unsheathes his knife
the shiny white belly, sliced, laid open
The fish, brave enough not to make a sound

Seagulls crowd closer with their gluttony
to the steaming guts, gritty with sand

Transformative Motion

                          Come! Look at this. Hurry!

Her excitement is of a dog
that has tree-trapped a coon

I walk fast through the soggy sand
to reach her

There in the sand, a Portuguese Man-of-War
only it's not blue, it's gray, a gray bubble-like body
with a twenty-inch stinger

Could this be the gray line, visible
for all to see? Is the search over?

                        She answers: Being that this is the North Pacific
                                    I'd say that this Man-of-War
                                    was caught in a southern current
                                    that dragged it to the cold north
                                    turning it gray as it crossed over

Still naked, she picks up the dead jellyfish
The wind gives flight to its stinger and like hot glue
it attaches to her left calf. She screams
as the fiery toxins burn her skin

She throws the jellyfish to the ground
and in a painful swagger heads to the salty water
then stops, squats, pees in her hand
and rubs it into the fiery wound

I stare at her injury then at the dead jellyfish
wanting so much for its stinger to be *the* gray line
I'm not afraid to imagine
I dig a hole, pick it up and bury it

She's breathing less heavily now
as the urine neutralized the acidic stab

I sit close to her, inhaling the alluring gaminess in her scent
Her eyes are teary. I take her in my arms. She spreads her legs
Our bodies copulate, and this transformative motion releases
her misery

The Murderer Of Fish

Everyone is capable of transformation
of detaching from what is not worthy

We must rid the mind of its thrashings

I lack words to convince the ignorant
that the gray line's nuances were designed
for control between light and dark
that will fade both to gray
leaving the universe in a bland state
without spiritual forces

Life and death will be enclosed
in gray. Such pity: gray
will be mundane and faster than light

If denouncement of the worthless
is not achieved, every mind will go cuckoo

                Wake up …

I hear her voice with its pleasant landscape
of sounds. I open my eyes, turn my head and look north

The murderer of fish is sitting in his beach chair
facing us, binoculars to his eyes: Surveillance

I sit up, then, facing him, kneel tall
so that my body blocks her nakedness
from his view and I piss in his direction

The murderer of fish gets up from his chair
flips me off and goes back to killing fish

                      She says: You were talking in your sleep
                            something about gray will be
                            mundane and faster than light

I try to remember the dream but my grogginess is brain cement
The sun is straight-up noon. The only evidence left of the jellyfish
is a quarter-inch burn on her left calf

Nobody Looks At Us

Nighttime. Back in the city
The day's heat crowns the evening
with spikes, thorns, whips
The concrete is bone on fire
The homeless smolder in clusters
Sky, a black flame
above high-wire transformers that crackle
and hiss

Near a liquor store, sprawled out
on his back, a grubby white man
has the claws of nightmare
dug into his frozen bearded expression

I lean down a bit to see if he's breathing
and sense the gray line's dominating pressure
around his neck
Nobody looks at us

A sudden gasp from the man
then he chuckles and pulls at his neck
as if loosening a tie. He sits up, leans
against the wall and falls back to sleep

                      Perhaps his dream was funny

I turn around and she is smiling

                      She continues: Sorry I'm late
                            So what will it be
                            wine or whiskey?

We take the whiskey to the edge of the city
into the forest to a bench
A rush of hot breeze is cooled by a multitude of leaves
and we find ourselves thirsty for liquor and sex

She, in a black tank top, flowing blood-red summer skirt
and black flip flops. Her raven hair twisted into a bun

Then like a bizarre dream my awareness shifts

Coiled around her injured leg
in spiral motion, as if
coming out of her quarter-inch wound,
the gray line seeks completion. Meaning:
the wound will become infected

                          She says: My injury burns

Pour whiskey on it

She did and the gray line turned to foam
and dissolved. She trembled

Just then, a hot breeze, like the dense breath
of lathered horses
and our bodies become the soil, the roots
the rain that breaks the heat

Mouth to mouth, this humid night drowns us
Our blood, intoxicated with whiskey

Her body, orchid's fragrance
slender paths
moist flame

My body, hard earth,
molten ore
hot springs

Mouth to mouth, body to body
we are nocturnal, nocturnal thirst, nocturnal oxygen
nocturnal crimson

The night is eternal

Omni Everything

Omnipresent

Omnipotent

Is and always has been

This night
so relaxing
A low clarinet
is chilled to an earthy nocturne
How pleasing

Omnipresent

Omnipotent

Is and always has been

Above the universe
all is gray
all consuming
all is something else's thoughts

Omnimute

Omni

Om

Little By Little

I've tried to color it
but it consumes all colors

I threw yellow at it
but yellow turned sickly

A sprinkle of white got through
only to disappear

Green curled at the edges, dissolved
Blue bruised and rotted

Though gray likes red
Red looks good with gray

Little by little
one after another
minds will go cuckoo

Something Else's Thoughts

Darkness grows gray
then bright
then dark
again turning gray

We are two parts of gray's polarities:
the simple and complex,
the sound, soundless,
black, white

I sense everything is beginning:
the before-world, after-world
the open entrance, closed entrance

My thoughts have become something else's thoughts
because I never know what I'm thinking or worse, why
was I thinking it?

I want to be ordinary, mundane, a basic pebble
an empty soul with no opinion
I hear talking inside my head
but it's not my voice:

Every cloud quivers to be rain
every rain falls to be an ocean
every ocean becomes a cloud

I answer without thinking:
Yes. No. But never maybe

Should I speak or should I listen?

Been Dreaming Too Long

Open eyes: birds, flowers, leaves, vines,
shedding eucalyptus. The sun,
groping the middle of the trees
A sketch of warmth lies around

My body stirs. Sitting up
I notice a note stuck to the bench with pine pitch
the empty whiskey bottle on the ground

                     Note reads: Gone to the clinic
                               for antibiotics
                               See you at the coast

I've been dreaming for too long about arrivals
departures, stagnation. No, that's not exactly it
it's more about something above the universe

Near the brook, a bar of soap, a washcloth,
                             another note: I figured we may need this

Sitting in a pool of cold water
I ask myself: Is it me or is creation blind?
Or what dominance is above the universe?
Will only gray remain after the universe dies?

Looking up I sense the gray line strung from treetop to treetop
as if a WEB, listening

A red leaf on the ground is a fallen star
The wood of each tree, a Brodsky poem

Another leaf spins, twirls, falls, lands
mute

I dress and walk into the city

Somewhere In My Head

I am here in skin, my shadow
shows me this

Heavy, dark, I haul it through the city's
gray slumber. Sharp metallic heat
carves fire into the walls

Stifling reflections, painful glare: Radiation

Somewhere in my head I'm beginning to hear light
and to hear clouds

Enter a pub: Void of people. On the bar,
a shot of whiskey, a lit cig. The stool is empty.
Turn to look at the room: Mr. Serling's shadow
is sitting in a corner booth. Behind me there's a cough.
I turn. The whiskey glass is empty, the cig gone.

I walk over to Serling's shadow. The closer I get to it
the more it fades to gray. When I reach it, it's gone.

Turn back toward the bar: There's a shadow
of a tall fat man with a round bald head sitting on the stool.
The shadow drinks the whiskey, smokes the cig.

I walk toward the shadow and reaching it extend my hand
to touch it, only to find it solid. I shudder as if touching
dried, black blood.

I move toward the door, walk outside. Nothing but shadows
from invisible people, trees, cars, animals and a shadow of
an invisible kite in flight. The shadow is a letter from above the universe.

> It reads: Where do you come from?
> Where is your shadow?

I look and I am without shadow.
The light is noisy. The scattering clouds are noisy.

                        I hear a voice: Rise and ascend.

I want to answer but my throat is a dry, crusted cave.

The Key Holders

... not because grief
              is without hope

not because change
              is led by thought

not because waves
              are children of oceans

a canvas filled with sand
              the stern broken

the fever, cottonmouth, sound bites
              gray light touches me
                            gray clouds are noisy ...

I wake up. The ocean is turbulent this time of year
like group chanting after a disaster
or group prayers that have become a whole sound

She is naked, standing close to the water and seems to have
overcome her fear of the massive breakers

The sun is three-quarters into late noon
My squinting eyes are tortured by the brightness

It is said that dreams are the key holders
to that which shapes our lives
to that which we have lost or never had
or what we are destined to become
yet I cannot remember
which direction to take or which hope holds certainty

If I hurt then I hold my hurt guarded
as if feeling nothing. An achromatic silence overtakes me

Part Five
The Way

The Way

Then she's yelling and pointing,
running back and forth along the water's edge

Beyond the aggressive breakers, diving and surfacing
like a patrolling submarine guarding the coastline, a gray whale.
When it spouts from its two blowholes,

two gray lines shoot in a V-pattern five hundred feet into the sky
as if an eruption of otherworldly oil
and her absolute joy announces the beauty of this creature's
presence and power

Much like a Taoist, the gray whale knows *The Way*
and never fails to pull its weight
or to achieve bliss in the wake of extinction

A cool pastel mist forms her nakedness
into layers of spectral skin. Her dark nipples,
hard glistening minerals that point to the sky
Her lengthy hair trails behind, like black flames
as she runs along the waterline trying to keep up of with the creature

The whale spouts again. Two more gray lines shoot so far into the sky
that they form one line that wraps around an Americana jet
on its descent

The jet drops quickly then pulls out of its fall and in a vertical climb
heads straight up only to turn downward and nose dive
three thousand feet into the ocean
There was no crash, no explosion, no broken off parts, no wake
It simply vanished

Against the horizon the gray whale is a silhouette
until it vanished, too

In the aftermath, the massive breakers sound like group chanting
in the wake of disaster and everything becomes jagged noise
like the crackling of a transformer moments before it explodes

I look beyond the breakers and sense the gray line in full-length
floating, like skin peeled from a gray whale

She is on her knees in disbelief.
Along the horizon, with a hiss and a bit of smoke
the sun dips into the ocean and in a truly uncanny way
darkness, like slow syrup, pours over the land

Cross-Legged In Meditation

The sudden gray mesh of clouds is a snag
that hooks one's deepest fear
In this state of unease
I realize we've been elbowed out of our coastline
by the bizarre disappearance
of Americana Flight 703

The sky is filled with helicopters, searchlights, small planes
and the water is crowded with search boats, diving bells
and frogmen.

The Coast Guard is blasting instructions
from megaphones and the coastline
for five-hundred yards in both directions
is flooded by halogen lamps
and the air is filled with nauseating diesel
while the media amplifies the emotions of those
watching this misfortune on television

The coast is littered with debris and the sand is rutted
with millions of footprints

At the bottom of the dunes in gray robes
a contingent of Taoist monks sit cross-legged in meditation
One of their comrades perished in the vanishing

All the while, along the horizon, the gray line floats
on its back, like a content sea otter

Should I feel something, anything
over the vanishing of 427 strangers?
It's easy to dismiss when the missing
are not yours

The Box

It is easy to dismiss
when the missing are not yours
still I search for sympathy
empathy, any human feelings.
I come up empty

For those who have lost loved ones
they are now memories:
memories will turn gray
memories will vanish in the gray future
memories will die inside of gray

We sit high up in the dunes
in an outcrop of bushes, not wanting to be noticed
not wanting to be questioned, not wanting to be interviewed
only to be left alone

This is day three of the search.
The coast is crowded with gawking strangers,
hyper media personal and sobbing relatives
of the missing

Nothing has been found
no jet, no jet parts, no bodies, simply nothing

703 crossed the sea's *Twilight Zone*
falling into strange collective thoughts,
into an icy cavity, into a dark watery-thicket beyond the gray line

It's late noon. She has been quiet and motionless the entire time
as if her body is a tranquilizer
We've slept very little

Through a bullhorn the supervisor of this operation
                announces: Sadly, I must say that this search is over
                        and may God care for your loved ones.
                        Amen.

Along the horizon the gray line reclines on its back
bobbing up and down on top of the Black Box

The captain's voice can be heard: 911 ... 911 ... everything is gray ...
mayday, mayday ...

There is no up, no down, no sideways, no heaven ... no ...

Then the gray line wraps around *The Box*. Together,
they disappear into the open mouth of the sea

Clouds Rub Against It

Slowly the moon rises like an alabaster balloon
and tries to push the gray cloud-cover apart

Without a sense of storm
lightning rips the sky like a throat infection
burning, crackling, hissing
In the distance thunder booms
its eerie canons
as if migrating from my chest

There is no wind, not even a breeze
The air feels strange, as if it's watching us

Lightning rips, more cannons, then
from the remaining gray clouds a warm rain breaks
with drops the size of pin balls denting the sand
and leaving marks, as if each drop were a clubfoot

She pulls closer to me, trembles then moans.
I cover her with my body. The air
becomes hot, humid, and the evening darkens
as the moon is ploughed under by gray clouds
You can hear squeaking as the clouds rub against it
then consume it

The rain's stimulating touch fondles our nakedness

Beneath me she is a water lily spreading her petals
and I, a hummingbird penetrating the petals
until I reach wet pollen. Throughout the night
we slow fuck in the sand
sleeping and waking and fucking
sleeping and waking and …

I feel something touch my back. I turn around …

A Colorless Prism

... I turn around. A young Taoist monk in freakish stillness
stares at us with unblinking, empty eyes, and, without having noticed,
the moon is visible again. The sky, a perfect forecast

The monk's baldhead glistens. His gray robe is littered
with ocean debris. The monk stands motionless, as if a crested wave
that cannot break

Then his eyes close, pop open, close, pop open ...
like the mechanical eyes of old-time dolls
I sense the gray line is under his robe, wrapped around his chest
constricting him from moving, causing his eyes to pop open and to snap
shut

                The young monk speaks
                in a low voice
                in fragments: Stars Fell
                          Gray Galaxy
                          Gray Kingdom
                          Gray Plummet
                          Strange Gray
                          Gray Matter
                          gray cells ... brain ... cells ...
                          ... yin ... gray ...

                yang

                I am tired of death
                and of life

                Tell me ... Brother ... is
                ... the World better?

Is the World better than what?

The monk speaks again:
>
> Yes, Brother, you are understood
> Yes, you will bleed
> like a colorless prism
> Yes, Eternity is here
> All is gray … all … gray

As If Only Beginning

They disappeared, each nonexistent face
disappeared in the clime of their own lust.
Still, I see them, invisible, bodies
of intercourse, shifting mouths of drool.

Something caresses me, a longing, lifeless
hand. Foam on the tip of its fingers, clearly
alive. Nameless, it pursues me with aggressive
foreplay, halfway between love and hatred.

There's an inward flight of paranoia, frozen
like plastic screams. Half of this gray scene
is over. Still it's lodged emotively inside
my body, as if only beginning.

Everything is old and faded, laboring or stillborn.
Somebody breaks bread. It begins to rain.
Whose fluid is running down my leg?

Somebody's life howls in distress, an echo
turns into a long alley where three dimensional
surrealism turns into horrible realism.

Grief, a mass of wind brought to life by cobwebs,
heavy gray light, gray pain,
flowers dying in sickly gray snow.

A disjointed body is conscious, whispering:
Look behind you. Behind you ...

Motion Unknown

Gray
Grayer
Grayness germinates, multiplies
becomes numerous
becomes full becomes heavy
in this world and others
becomes air
fire
water
becomes earth
It is one portion
then two
then three and four portions
It is consistent in inconsistency
visible in its apparition
without origin
without sound
without giving
it pushes and pulls
motion unknown
tide is high
ocean chokes
waves cannot swim
After the current drowns them
they break above the universe

        The monk speaks:
        Brother, I have forgotten this world and the other
        The dust of this dirge is tone deaf
        Look behind you ...

Above The Universe

Far away, another wind
Somewhere, rain I cannot feel
I shudder from bone to bone
Transparent motionless waves
slice the air
Dizzy seagulls
collapse on the sand
heads bobbing like limp sadness
And far beyond
above the universe
spread evenly throughout
the gray line stretches and shapes
like a jet's broken body falling to the sea
The sun's solar brilliance dims
like a dead firefly
The gray sun is disturbingly beautiful
a dull heart
gray flames
Static, a familiar noise
a whir of wings in a glass jar
burning the oxygen
the bug inhales
exhales
a gray toxin
tighter tighter
bug suffocates

Every Dream Is A Crowded World

Because the world is lost
within its own crowd
everything sacred is obscene
everything holy is disrespectful
Because the wind blows backwards
everything happens to not happen
dust rises never falls
The wind's mouth
a dilated crusted vent
Because dying is a memory
a place inside earth from earth
to earth before earth
every death is desirous
every death is a host
Because dreams are inscriptions
from yesterday's existence
from today's psychosis
from tomorrow's dementia
every dream is a crowded world

                      The monk speaks: Beyond the gray line
                                      it is quiet
                                        The current sings to itself
                                        I try to remember
                                        but why
                                        You are amongst us
                                        now

Suddenly, static, and then a familiar noise
like the whir of wings in a glass jar

I ... cannot ... breathe ...

Part Six

Incomplete

Empty You, Empty Me

Eyes focus. An old spider's web,
a net for dehydrated things, like spent seeds
ashen and speckled black
I watch it quiver, a tattered tissue
in a draft

I'm trying to collect my thoughts, feeling neglected memories
inscribed on my DNA
Warm wind crosses my face
a dry monsoon
The shack's door is open. I hear the ocean
and smell burning wood, cooked fish

Standing in the doorway looking out
under a strong sun, I see her lounging nude
in the sand next to a small fire and a pan of sizzling fish

The breakers smack steadily against the cliffs
The beach is deserted as far as eyes can see

                She sees me, smiles and says:
                      Hey! The dead hath risen
                      You've been sleeping for a day and a half
                      I went to the city, bought some green apples
                      did our laundry. That was a lot of whiskey
                      we poured down. You passed out on the cot
                      I brought back fresh water for bathing

What happened to the debris and the millions of footprints
in the sand?
— my mouth, as dry as thirsty caves. Eyes burning.

She smiles and answers but I can't hear her over the boom
of another wave. She goes back to sunbathing

Fish? But we're vegan.

The beach, the water, seem far away, as if too far.

The sun torches it with white-hot, as if too hot to touch.
I stagger toward the waterline, turn to look back
She's kneeling up and waving, as if waving good-bye
Then it's odd because she's saying something
and from this far distance I can hear her over more wave-smacks

                        She says: It's really spellbinding here
                                Don't worry
                                the rain keeps it away

Her nakedness is silken fabric that causes my nakedness
to erect, yet from the whiskey
my desire is dead

                        She continues:
                            If I knew what you want
                            or need
                            If I knew what I want
                            or need
                            The empty you
                            the empty me
                            One moment of delusion
                            is all it takes

Huh?

I continue to stagger to the waterline, feeling myself melting
under the blazing pressure and then I see it, the gray line
using the ocean as a climbing gym

I look back, she is standing and yelling down to me: Imagine rain!

I watch salt separate from the water
and lift into the air
as if a warning. Watching it form
into a journey of bitter light

It's a bizarre image: salt inside air

Now the sky is filled with slow-motion-gliding gray pelicans
that make me feel an ancient loneliness
The ocean is soundless, like music that has paused

Whose alteration is this?

— worthless sand dollars, gray sea stars, my shadow on the ocean floor
a sea urchin that aches with dullness, the soundless waves

Clouds cantilever over the pelicans
In its damp ghostly gown an oncoming fog unravels its threads
and grows chilly

With two semitones, a wave breaks and crashes in d-diminished 3rd
wracking my nerves, like any wicked chord that sustains beyond
its audible voicing

I move back from the waterline and the gray line expands
in the air. The coast is ruled by seagulls and policed
by sandpipers. The gliding pelicans are fluff
floating from a windless resurrection

I turn, look back at the shack, the fire. She's nowhere
to be seen. I turn back to the ocean and see her
standing close to the water's edge. The gray line
is coiled around her left ankle seeking completion

I move closer to her, press my nakedness to the back of hers
and kiss the nape of her neck. She shudders, the gray line contracts

My eyes flutter and my mouth fills with what tastes like salt
only it's her tongue. Her body glows as she guides my body
into hers and like two colliding waves we release, break into foam
release again, spill more foam

My eyes flutter

REM

What is it that sometimes makes memory a lead ball?

In writing this, I do not know why. In speaking of this
I cannot. In imagining this, what remains as real
and where will imagination take me?

The ocean is a city strung with seaweed and wired
with negative ions. The ionic minerals wash into our brains
by way of osmosis, which lightens the lead load of melancholy

The gray line's intent: to suck negative ions from the water
to suck them from our bodies, to keep us melancholic, confused,
and submissive.

The ocean is a voice whose wet grammar forms deep-sea-syllables:
Twi-Light-Zone, Si-Lence, Dr-Owned, Bloa-Ted …
it speaks of everything lost

The ocean is a voice that supplies syllables to the whales
Even in silence their bodies are prose pressed into
the water's weight, into the salt, into the emptiness between
light and dark: Twilight Zone / Gray Zone

It's time to remember. I'm barefoot. Sand dabs stick to my feet
In my mouth, her bliss: sultry, steamy, a starfish
then a clam expelling foam, juice, salt and heat
A river of honey-milk

> She whispers: Think rain
>   Think long lasting rain

It's pouring electric water and the gray line latches onto the rain
traveling into the city, using it like public transit

The rain keeps it away? She's grinning. Rapid Eye Movement …

A Living Gray

Gray (or grey): intermediate shade between black and white

Gray Water

    Graybar

        Gray Matter

            Gray Cells

Cell Gray

Gray Matter (or grey matter [lat. Substantia grisea])
    a major component of the central nervous system

Gray Cells: nerve cells that are gray from a concentration of mitochondria and their close proximity to blood vessels

        C. G. Jung says: Well done
            You are a fine student

Applause ... louder ... louder ...

gray noise ... Dr. Jung walks away from the podium

applause ... louder ... louder ...

        then Dr. Jung says: Even with this information
            that the sun shares about light
            the skin-tissue of clouds
            is gray: gray water, gray air
            sorrowful gray thoughts
            a liquid gray
            that drips like melting matter.

My Indignity, My Delusion?

I cough, cough again and wake up: the air is gray
dead gray, the rain is gray, a living gray

and it's coming down like a charge of warriors
The rain hits the shack's tin roof with the sound
of a massive crowd's applause.

We're huddled together on the cot. A cold breeze
leaks through the air. Ocean's voice is stentorian.
Curled closely together, our naked bodies shiver.

She's in deep sleep.

I feel like a sick dodo dragging myself through these thoughts,
these thoughts without direction,
these thoughts that are puzzle pieces to nothing
these thought that are something else's thoughts.

The chilled light that covers our bodies is a gray drift
of blunt light that seems to not exist, like past participles,
gone, been.

Perhaps I, too, am a past participle, a used fragment, sediment,
an incertitude that began within itself and has no chance of changing.
That lives without a will to live.

What is it that I need to explain, that I must say, that haunts me
like mud holding me down?

Gray light through the window falls on green apples in a bowl
on the table. They glow a greenish-gray aura, like that of
a dying child's eyes. Now the heavy rain is a bustling city.

Should I pretend that it's not like this, that everything is
my dissatisfaction, my indignity, my delusion?

Broken #2

That which is broken works
for those who want it broken

Can I exist like this
can anybody live this way

knowing that within our minds
a sub-mind of deep surveillance
creates eyes inside one's privacy?

And where does it stop, what else will we lose?
What more does Tight-Mind want?

I'm already tired of the future
because so many people will be missing

The gray line, the outline, the underline, borderline
boundary line, edge line, demarcation line, the firing line:

up against a gray wall …

Compassion and empathy
are strangers in dreams. Treeless nature
is clogged with wireless eyes and ears

Maybe there is another world where
dreams are dreams are never nightmares
somewhere above the universe

Incomplete

Is existence trivial
lifeless
pointless
worthless

                                        The gray line says:
                                      dreams are empty
                                      existence is empty

We are incomplete
Here
we grow old

Yes we grow
as death grows
Yes

Part Seven

Therapy

I say: To imagine the gray line is to understand your death,
    a slow uncorking of chardonnay.

C. G. Jung:
*A person should follow his instinct and embrace myth over reason
for reason shows him nothing but the dark pit into which he is
descending. Myth can conjure other images for him, helpful and
enriching pictures of life in the land of the dead.*

Job 30:27-31
My heart is troubled and restless.
Days of suffering torment me
I walk in gloom, without sunlight.
I stand in the public square crying for help.
I am considered a brother to jackals,
a companion to owls.
My skin has turned dark,
my bones burn with fever.
My harp plays sad music,
my flute accompanies those who weep.

C. G. Jung: *What you resist persists.*

Job 33:15-17
In dreams, in visions of the night, when sleep falls on people
in their beds
there may be terrifying warnings
that could turn them from wrongdoing and keep them from pride.

C. G. Jung:
*Through pride we deceive ourselves,
and below the surface of the conscience
a small voice says to us, something is out of tune.*

Daniel 4:5
What I saw in a dream made me fearful and,
as I lay on my bed, these fantasies and visions
kept alarming me.

C. G. Jung:
*Knowing your own darkness is the best method
for dealing with the darkness of others.*

Ecclesiastes 5:3
A dream comes when there are many cares,
and many words mark the speech of a fool.

C. G. Jung:
*Until you make the unconscious conscious,
it will direct your life and you will call it fate.*

Psalm 37:1
Do not fret because of those who are evil
or be envious of those who do wrong,
for, like the grass, they will soon wither,
like green plants, they will soon die.

C. G. Jung:
*Even a happy life cannot be without a measure of darkness,
and the word happy would lose its meaning if it were not
balanced by sadness. It is far better to take things as they
come, with patience and equanimity.*

Matthew 6:25
Therefore I tell you, do not worry about your life,
or what you will eat or drink, or about your body,
or what you will wear. Is not life more than food,
the body more than clothes?

C. G. Jung:
*Nobody, as long as he moves among
the chaotic currents of life, is without trouble.*

James 1:6
But when you ask, you must believe
and not doubt, because the one who doubts
is like a wave of the sea, blown and tossed by the wind.

C. G. Jung:
*A man who has not passed through the inferno of his passions
has never overcome them. As far as we can discern,
the purpose of human existence is to kindle a light
in the darkness of mere being. Everything that irritates us
about others can lead us to an understanding of ourselves.*

I Thessalonians 4:11
To make it your ambition to lead a quiet life,
you should mind your own business
and work with your hands ...

C. G. Jung:
Sometimes you have to do something unforgivable
just to be able to go on living and I am convinced
that it is hygienic – if I may use the word –
to discover in death a goal toward which one can strive,
and that shrinking away from it is something unhealthy

and abnormal, which robs the second half of life of its purpose.

She whispers:
Death, the forgotten comfort.

Part Eight

Dreams

Our truest life is when we are in dreams awake

— Henry David Thoreau

Gray: This indicates feelings of a dull existence, a daily round without excitement. It also indicates lack of clarity, indecision or blurring of distinctions. Like fog, it suggests not being able to see clearly.

Dreaming of gray could symbolize weakness or lack of direction in one's life. This may also denote one cannot decide upon a path to take, as in hazy. Gray also represents a hidden deception or being deceived by a false doctrine.

Gray may indicate fear, fright, depression, ambivalence and confusion. One may feel emotionally distant, isolated or detached.

Gray represents old age or depression. As an intermediate between black and white, gray may symbolize an unclear state of mind where distinctions are blurred, where one has difficulty seeing where they are going, or one has lost a sense of direction.

Nudity: Being naked in a dream can indicate feelings of freedom, innocence and wholeness especially when accompanied by happiness. These dreams can symbolize complete self-acceptance, presenting the whole self to the world without shame.

Being naked in a dream can also an indicate that one has set unrealistic goals where one has no way of meeting them.

Sex: Sexual dreams are not necessarily about sex. Often they are about how we perceive people or how we think others perceive us. To construct a framework for interpreting sexual dreams it is important to identify who is in the dream and how we feel about the experiences.

The sexual dream may announce the presence of a transformative process either emotionally or spiritually.

Weather: Weather dreams often portray what is going on in our inner landscape using settings familiar in the outer world. A focus on the weather will represent the inner climate. If it is raining you may need to express your emotions more. If it is sunny the dream can be exploring what will lead to greater happiness. If it is windy we may need to let go of outdated ideas.

Rain: Rain is a positive symbol indicating a solution to a certain problem. Rain and storms are good signs. The storm represents an important solution for a problem. Rain shows that you have found the answer that you were looking for. The unconscious mind will help you understand what you have found and why this finding will help you solve your problems.

Rain can also be a prediction. You may be about to discover what you need. In this case the dream symbol prepares you for finding a solution. It works like an alert.

A dream about rain or a storm may also make you pay attention to your reality without forgetting that you are looking for a solution. You will have the attitude of a researcher without being disconnected from your reality. Rain reminds you that you have to pay attention to details in order to find the solution.

Sand Dunes: Dreaming of sand dunes portends poverty, unhappiness or insignificant troubles. Sand dunes suggest closeness to family and spirituality. Sand dunes are signs that a hypocritical person will try to influence you. Dreaming of sand foretells instability or signifies emotion between yourself and someone of the opposite sex. Sand dunes indicate that an uncertain relationship in your life will disturb you and this is a reminder to not waste your energy on it. Walking on sand dunes means the deals you are into at the moment are unsafe.

To see a sand dune in your dream signifies your desires to be sheltered from the bitterness of reality.

Shack: A shack symbolizes an untapped potential. One should be more creative and take initiative.

The Beach: To be near the sea is connected to emotions. The beach is a place where emotions connect with water, plus the material world, symbolic of the sand, come together. This dream shows that you are keeping strong feelings inside and not letting them out.

Pelicans: Dreams of pelicans may illustrate the process of realization in which new insights emerge, die, go back into the unconscious and return again — C. G. Jung

Pelicans can be meaningful as they represent an animal that needs water. The unconscious is often symbolized in dreams as water. Humans, like pelicans, need an intimate relationship with water in order to live a balanced life — Dr. J. Howlin (Jungian Psychologist)

Shadows: The repressed aspect of ourselves, the part of our self that we do not want the world to see. It symbolizes weakness, fear or anger. Shadows are represented as stalkers, murderers, bullies, or pursuers and their appearances can often make one angry or scared. They force us to confront things that we do not want to. We must learn to accept the shadow, as its messages are often for our own good even though it may not be mmediately apparent — C. G. Jung

Whales: We associate whales with tranquility so dreams about them will link to feelings which touch on this theme or that one has experienced something spiritual. One may have felt a real sense of connection with someone or maybe one is simply trying to be calm but failed. Whales symbolize a wish to stay calm.

Plane Crash: A plane crash suggests one is anxious about failure as in having planned a project that doesn't get you where you thought it would and is accompanied by a fear that things will end badly. Plane-crash dreams are common during recessions and can be directly translated as someone worrying about finances. This dream can also relate to important projects or goals where there is fear over not reaching a successful completion.

Jellyfish: Jellyfish are not easily seen with tentacles that sting. They can portray fear of delving beneath the surface to trace the roots of your feelings. Their transparent skin associates them with the idea that you may be thin skinned in your emotional interactions. You may have vague sensations of fear that cause you to be over reactive.

Alcohol: Dreams of drinking alcohol may be exploring the idea of alcohol dependency. We usually dream of what we are not acknowledging. Being drunk can also suggest feelings of exhilaration that you are not expressing during waking life. The purpose of dreaming is to face the truth about what we fail to acknowledge; to help us express our true nature. If drunk in a dream, one may have lost their feelings of sensitivity when relating to their environment.

Famous People: Dreaming about famous people is about seeking inspiration or some characteristic that is associated with that celebrity, or seeking accomplishment, good health or empowerment.

City: To be in a city signifies a social environment and sense of community. If you dream of a big city then it suggests that you need to develop closer ties and relationships because you are feeling alienated and alone. To dream that you are in a deserted city indicates that you feel rejected by those around you.

Dead Fish: A dead fish may signify disappointment and loss. This loss may be associated with power, wealth, or spirituality in one's life. Since fish are associated with the unconscious, a dead fish may symbolize something old giving way to new growth.

Binoculars: Binoculars represents your interest in the future. Looking ahead or being concerned about what might happen.

Starfish: A starfish indicates that you need to revive yourself spiritually and emotionally. It may also mean that you need to assess a situation thoroughly before you come to a conclusion.

Monks: To see monks signifies inner faith and spiritual strength. A monk symbolizes your spiritual side. It indicates that although you are operating in the secular world, you have spiritual depth to your nature.

Awake Within Dreams: Being awake within a dream is a phenomenon. They are vivid dreams in which you are convinced that you have woken up in physical reality. The dream of being awake suggests a level of self-awareness. Yet many false awakenings go unrecognized or are assumed to be a waking reality where there is no awareness that it is a dream. It reveals the remarkable capacity of the sleeping brain to emulate reality.

Who looks outside, dreams.
Who looks inside, awakens.

— C. G. Jung

Acknowledgements

My gratitude to the following publications where these poems first appeared:

Indian River Review: "Something Else's Thoughts"

The Bombay Review (India): "Every Dream Is A Crowded World"

Record Magazine: "Language"

Abbreviate Journal: "Never A Sky Clear Enough", "Where Ever I Was"

Eunoia Review (Singapore): "Misdirected", "The Vanishing Of Differences"

Dead Snakes Magazine: "Disheveled Boats", "Everyday Motion", " Imperfection"

Diverse Voices Quarterly: "Weather Predicts Everything"

Jellyfish Whispers: "Myth"

Literature Today (India): "Without Voice Without Living"

New Mystics Magazine: "We Turn Into Earth"

Futures Trading: "Words Of Dreams", "Pass Through The Center"

Spillwords Magazine (Poland): "Broken #2"

Duane's PoeTree Journal: "Incomplete", "The Balance Between"

Mad Swirl Magazine: "I Say Dream Only"

Medusa's Kitchen: "Above The Universe", "As If Only Beginning", "Broken"
          "The Drunkeness In Its Eyes"

An unending thank you to my longtime friend and writer Michael Grotsky for his perceptive introduction which explains everything by saying nothing.

A special hat tip to my longtime friend and editor Ron Tompkins and for his insightful suggestions and questions concerning some of the concepts and phrases that make up *Something Else's Thoughts*.

I wish to express my appreciation to these poets from the poetry critique group, *The Lounge:* Paul Larner, Heather Browne, Doug Sandvick, David Emmanual, Sola Oyefara, Rich Unger, Stephen Edward Godfrey, Lotta Hellron, Kerri Rochell, Munia Kahn, Qaanita Khalid, Joshua Yaw Koranteng, Kimberly Dickens, Chad Repko, and Diana Baker-Vevang, whom in countless ways shaped many of these poems from draft to finish with their fine suggestions.

Last, and certainly not least, my unending appreciation to publishers Dustin Pickering and Z.M. Wise for believing in this manuscript and for taking this project into book form. And to graphic designer Glynn Irby for his work on the spine, for setting up the files for the printer, and for his unending patients with my nitpicking fussiness over so many details.

NOTE: "Misdirected" was first published as "If Truth Is Misspelled"

"I Say Dream Only" was also published in Duane's PoeTree Journal

The Biblical quotes and the dream evaluations are from various WEB sources, leaving the Author and the Publishers in no way responsible for inaccuracies or accuracies concerning these interpretations.

Author

For information about the author

Visit:

Words Of Dahlusion

dahlusion.wordpress.com

More Books by Dah

The Opening
CTU Publishing Group, 2018

Say This In A Whisper
Red Wolf Editions, 2017

The Translator
Transcendent Zero Press, 2015

If You Have One Moment
Stillpoint Books, 2015

The Second Coming
Stillpoint Books, 2012

In Forbidden Language
Stillpoint Books, 2010

Contact

Email: dahlusion@yahoo.com

Web Site: dahlusion.wordpress.com

Twitter: @dahlusion

Tumblr: Dahlusion

Linked In

Facebook: Art Of Dahlusion

Google: dahlusion

www.ingramcontent.com/pod-product-compliance
Lightning Source LLC
Chambersburg PA
CBHW071309060426
42444CB00034B/1749